THE
HEAVENLY ZOO

Legends and Tales of the Stars

Retold by
ALISON LURIE

With pictures by
MONIKA BEISNER

A Sunburst Book
Farrar, Straus and Giroux

CONTENTS

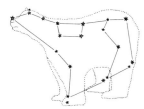
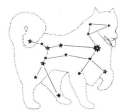
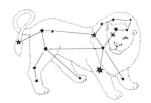

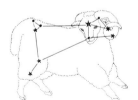

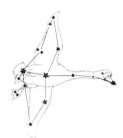

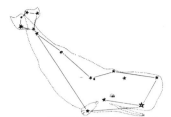

THE WHALE 42

THE FISHES 45

THE BULL 50

THE WOLF 53

THE SEA-GOAT 56

THE DOVE 59

Preface

From the earliest times people have looked at the night sky and tried to understand what they saw there. Long before anyone knew that the stars were great burning globes of gas many millions of miles from the earth and from one another, men and women saw the sky as full of magical pictures outlined with points of light.

What shapes ancient people saw in the sky depended on who and where they were. Thus the group of stars that we call the Big Dipper, which is part of the Great Bear, was known to the Egyptians as the Car of Osiris, to the Norse as Odin's Wagon, and in Britain first as King Arthur's Chariot and later as the Plough. Many of the pictures that we see today are very old. The constellation we call the Great Dog was first known as a dog five thousand years ago in Sumeria; Taurus the Bull was already a bull in Babylon and Egypt.

Our ancestors saw all sorts of things in the stars: men and women, gods and demons, rivers and ships. But what they saw most often were beasts, birds, and fish. And for most of these creatures there was a legend of how they came to be there. This book is a collection of such tales from all over the world. Many of them were told by the ancient Greeks and Romans; some can be read in the

Bible; others are from the Balkans, or Indonesia, or the American Indians. Some are heroic, some comic, some sad; but all full of the wonder we still feel when we look at the sky full of stars.

The Eagle

As the lion is the king of beasts, so the eagle is the king of birds, and the bird of kings. Long ago in Greece, there lived a great eagle called Aquila, who was the servant of Zeus, the king of the gods. Aquila stood near Zeus' throne on Mount Olympus, and bore the thunderbolts with which he struck those mortals who had broken his laws.

Now in Arcadia there had been born a child named Aesculapius, who was the son of the god Apollo and a mortal woman. As a boy he was given into the care of the centaur Chiron, who was half man and half horse, and Chiron taught him the arts of medicine and healing. So skilled did Aesculapius become that at last he was able not only to cure the sick but to revive those who had already died. One day as he was sitting in his garden a poisonous serpent appeared. Aesculapius killed the serpent, but as it lay dead another serpent came sliding out of the grass with a green herb in its mouth, which brought the dead one back to life. Aesculapius took some of the herb from the serpent, and thus gained the power to raise the dead.

When Pluto, the king of the Underworld who ruled over all departed souls, heard of this he was

much displeased. He went to Zeus and complained that if Aesculapius were not stopped he would soon empty the Underworld and people the earth with the dead. Zeus therefore sent Aquila to earth to strike Aesculapius with a thunderbolt. Then he set Aesculapius and his serpent among the stars, so that his wisdom and goodness might not be forgotten. Near him in the sky is Zeus' bird, Aquila the *Eagle,* poised as if to strike Aesculapius down.

The Great Bear

Long ago in Arcadia there lived a king named Lykaon who had a beautiful daughter called Callisto. The princess was a huntress and a follower of the virgin goddess Artemis and had sworn to her that she would never love any man. But one hot summer afternoon while Callisto was sleeping under a tree in the forest, Zeus, the king of the gods, saw her and fell in love with her. At first, remembering her promise, Callisto resisted him; but presently she returned his love.

When Artemis' other maidens learned what Callisto had done, they would hunt and play with her no longer. Sad and lonely, she wandered off into the woods of Arcadia, where there were no people, only wolves and bears and other wild beasts. There she gave birth to a baby boy whom she named Arcas.

Now when the queen of the gods, Hera, heard what had happened she became jealous. She descended to earth and appeared before Callisto, full of rage. Calling out words of power, she flung her to the ground. At once the princess's robes dropped from her, her arms and legs thickened and became shaggy with fur, and her face lengthened into a muzzle. She tried to beg for mercy, but her

voice had changed into a roar; she had become a great white bear.

Her little boy, Arcas, did not know her any more; he screamed and ran away out of the forest into the open fields. There he was found and adopted by a kind farmer. Callisto could not follow him, but had to hide deep in the woods to escape the hunters, her former companions.

As Arcas grew up he inherited his mother's skill at hunting with bow and arrow. He ranged further and further into the great forest, and at last one day he came upon Callisto. When she recognized her son she forgot her bear's shape and ran to hug him, growling with joy. Arcas thought he was being attacked, and drew his bow. He would have shot Callisto to the heart if Zeus, who sees all things, had not come to her rescue. Zeus seized the bear by her tail and swung her up among the stars. Then, so that Callisto might never again be separated from her son, he changed Arcas also into a bear, and tossed him too into the heavens, where they became the *Great Bear* and the Little Bear.

The Great Dog

Once upon a time in India there were five princes who left their kingdom to seek the kingdom of heaven. With them they took only food and drink for the journey; and the prince Yudistira brought his dog Svana.

Now besides Yudistira, who was the eldest, the brothers were Sahadeva the all-wise, who was learned beyond other men; Nakula the all-handsome, famed for his grace and beauty; Arjuna the all-powerful, who had never been defeated in any contest of arms; and Bhima the all-joyful, known far and wide for his good temper and love of pleasure.

So they set forth, and journeyed many days and many nights. Presently they came to a fair, where music was playing and people were drinking and dancing and feasting. Some of them saw Bhima the all-joyful, and called out for him to come and join them. Bhima said to himself, "I will rest here today and be happy, and seek the kingdom of heaven tomorrow." So he entered into the dance. And Yudistira and his brothers Sahadeva and Nakula and Arjuna and his dog Svana went on without him.

They travelled for many days and many nights, till they came to a broad plain where a great army was drawn up in ranks facing the enemy. When the soldiers saw Arjuna the all-powerful they shouted out, summoning him to come and lead them into battle. Arjuna said to himself, "I will fight today for my country, and seek the kingdom of heaven tomorrow." So he joined the soldiers; and Yudistira and his brothers Sahadeva and Nakula and his dog Svana went on without him.

So they travelled for many days and nights, till they came to a magnificent palace surrounded by a garden full of flowers and fountains; and in this garden a beautiful princess was walking with her attendants. When she saw Nakula the all-handsome she was seized with love and longing, and she cried out for him to come nearer. Nakula too was struck with love, and said to himself, "I will stay with this princess today, and seek the kingdom of heaven tomorrow." So he went into the garden, and Yudistira and his brother Sahadeva and his dog Svana went on without him.

They journeyed on for many weary days and nights, until they came to a great temple. When the holy men who lived there saw Sahadeva the all-wise they ran out, inviting him to come and join them in prayer and study. And Sahadeva said to himself, "I will stay here today, and seek the kingdom of heaven tomorrow." So he went into

the temple, and Yudistira and his dog Svana went on without him.

At last Yudistira came to Mount Meru, which is the doorway to heaven. And Indra the Lord of Past and Present appeared before him, and invited him to ascend. Yudistira bowed low and replied, "Very willingly I will do so, if I may bring my dog Svana with me."

"That may not be," said Indra. "There is no place in heaven for dogs. Cast off this beast, and enter into eternal happiness."

"I cannot do that," said Yudistira. "I do not wish for any happiness for which I must cast off so dear a companion."

"You travelled on without your four brothers," said Indra. "Why will you not ascend to heaven without this dog?"

"My lord," replied Yudistira, "my brothers left me to follow the desires of their hearts. But Svana has given his heart to me; rather than renounce him I must renounce heaven."

"You have spoken well," said Indra. "Come in, and bring your dog with you." So Yudistira and Svana ascended into paradise; and Indra, in recognition of their devotion to each other, set in the sky the constellation of the *Great Dog,* whose central star Sirius is the brightest of all in the heavens.

The Lion

O nce there was a time when the heavens were disturbed. Stars left their places, comets shot across the sky, and a burning meteor fell from the moon and landed in the valley of Nemea in Greece in the shape of a golden lion. This beast, which was far larger and fiercer than any earthly lion, made its lair in a cave in the hills, and soon began to lay waste the countryside around, killing sheep and cattle, tearing up the fields of grain, and terrifying the people. The Nemean farmers tried to kill the lion, but its hide was so tough that no weapon would pierce it, and those who went out to hunt the beast were fortunate to return alive.

Month by month the lion grew larger and more terrible. At last Heracles, the great hero of the Greeks, was sent by his cousin King Eurystheus to slay the Nemean lion and bring back its skin. This was the first of the twelve dreadful tasks Heracles had to perform for the king.

So Heracles armed himself and went into the valley of Nemea. He searched first for someone who could tell him where the lion's cave was, but there was nobody in the fields or cottages: all the people had fled. Then he saw the lion returning from its day's hunting, spattered with blood. He

shot at it with his bow, but the arrows only bounced off and fell to the ground; then he came nearer and launched a spear, which when it hit the beast bent as if it had been made of lead. Finally Heracles struck at the lion with his club, but the animal did not even seem to feel the blows; it leaped straight upon him. Summoning up all his strength, Heracles put his hands around the lion's neck and began to choke it. When at last it was dead, he lifted the huge body onto his shoulders and carried it down the valley to show the farmers of Nemea that their enemy would trouble them no more.

When Heracles came to skin the lion, no knife would cut it, so he used one of its own claws. He did not give the hide to King Eurystheus; for his father Zeus, who had been watching, granted Heracles the right to wear it himself in honour of his victory. And the king of the gods also set in the sky the figure of a *Lion* made of stars, so that his son's great deed might be remembered always.

The Water-Serpent

Heracles was the son of Zeus and a mortal woman, called Alcmene. Even as a baby his strength and courage were prodigious. Hera, Zeus' wife, was jealous of her husband's child and plotted to kill him. She sent two snakes to attack Heracles in his cradle; but he seized them by their necks as if they were toys and choked them to death.

As a man, Heracles performed twelve impossible tasks known as the labours of Heracles. One of the most difficult of these was his battle with the Hydra, an enormous and terrible water-serpent which lived in the marshes of Lerna, emerging at night to devour both men and beasts. The Hydra had nine heads, each one equipped with sharp fangs; and what was worse, whenever one head was cut off, two new ones would grow in its place.

In preparation for his meeting with the Hydra, Heracles pulled up a great oak tree by its roots and shaped it into a club, which he set alight. Then he made his way to the marsh and called the Hydra. It crawled out of the mud, hissing with rage and spitting venom. Heracles raised his sword in one hand and his burning club in the other; and each time he chopped off one of the monster's heads he scorched the place with fire so that no more heads

could grow there. For thirty nights, so legend says, he fought with the serpent. At last he conquered it, and delivered the people of Lerna from its ravages.

In memory of his victory Zeus placed Heracles and his club among the stars. The *Water-Serpent* can also be seen there, as a long chain of stars winding across the sky near the constellation of the Lion.

The Dragon

Before our world was made, so it was written in ancient Babylon, there was no sky and no earth, only a waste and confusion of waters. The ruler of the fresh water was Apsu, and the ruler of the salt water was the she-dragon, Tiamat. They met and mingled together, and from them a race of gods was born.

Now as time passed the gods grew in strength and numbers, and rebelled against Apsu and Tiamat. When Apsu knew of this he determined to destroy them. But before he could do so, the god Ea cast a spell of sleep upon him, and slew him.

Then Tiamat the Dragon was enraged, and swore to be revenged upon the gods. So out of the salt water she created a race of monsters: poisonous serpents and ravening wolves and dragons breathing fire; fish men and scorpion men and men with claws and teeth like lions. Yet of all these monsters she herself was the most horrible, and the most invincible, for her mouth was seven miles wide, and her hide so thick that no weapon could pierce it.

Now when the gods saw Tiamat and her monsters preparing for battle they were struck with terror and despair. None dared to oppose her, save only for Marduk the son of Ea. Therefore the gods

honoured Marduk, set him upon their highest throne, and gave him power over all things.

Then Marduk prepared himself for battle. He made himself a great bow, the first ever known in the world, and a quiver full of arrows. Also he wove a net in which to trap Tiamat; and he called the four winds to him, North, South, East, and West, that each might hold one corner of the net. Next Marduk made the Seven Winds of Vengeance: the Hot Wind and the Cold Wind, the Whirlwind and the Sandstorm; the Fourfold Wind, the Sevenfold Wind, and the Destroying Tempest. He called them about him, mounted his chariot, and went forth boldly; and the other gods followed behind him. But when he drew near to Tiamat and saw how terrible she was, he faltered for a moment; and as for the other gods, they grew faint and dared go no further.

So alone Marduk went forward. When Tiamat shrieked with rage and rushed upon him, lashing her tail, he threw his net over her. Tiamat opened her terrible mouth to devour him; but the Hot Wind blew into it so that she could not close her jaws, and all the other Winds of Vengeance entered in, filling her belly, so that she grew weak. Marduk drew his bow, and shot an arrow down Tiamat's throat into her heart. She gave a great howl, and fell dead. Seeing this, the other monsters began to run off, but Marduk caught them and trampled them under foot.

After the battle was over, Marduk split Tiamat's huge body into two parts like a shellfish. From one half he created the earth, with its mountains and valleys; he separated the salt water from the fresh, and made great rivers flow into the sea. The other half he raised up, and of it he made the heavens, the dwelling-place of the gods.

There he set the sun and the moon and the stars, and ordered their motions, so that day might be separated from night, and summer from winter. And Marduk fastened the dome of heaven in place with the North Star, and round it he set a great *Dragon* in the likeness of Tiamat, to guard it for all eternity.

The Scorpion

Orion was one of the greatest of the Greek giants. Because he was the son of Poseidon, the god of the sea, he was as much at home in the water as on land. When he wished to get from one island to another he walked across on the bottom of the ocean; he was so tall that his head was always above the waves, and so large and broad that his travels caused high tides.

From childhood on Orion was famous for his beauty and his tremendous strength. He grew up to be a great hunter, able to track and slay all kinds of beasts with the help of his giant hound Sirius. When the island of Chios was oppressed and terrified by lions and wolves, Orion came to its assistance. He tracked down and destroyed every one, so that the people and their flocks could live in safety.

By the time Orion came to the large island of Crete, his fame was so great that Artemis, the goddess of the moon, invited him to go hunting with her. All went well until Orion, who had become vain of his skill, began to boast that he would soon have killed all the wild animals in Crete. Now the scorpion, who was listening, said to himself that this must not be. So he lay in wait for Orion, and stung him to death with his poisoned tail.

But Orion's spirit did not have to go down to dwell in the Underworld with the souls of ordinary mortals. The gods, who loved him, transported him instead to the sky, where he can be seen in his golden armour and sword-belt, holding up his golden shield, with his faithful dog Sirius at his heel. The scorpion who saved the wild animals of Crete was also raised into the heavens, and became a constellation in the southern sky.

Every night, as the *Scorpion* rises, Orion fades and vanishes.

The Crab

In the beginning of things, so they say in Malaysia, there was only one animal of each kind upon the earth, and they were far, far larger than animals are now. The First and Only Turtle was so big that when she crawled across the land her track became the bed of a river; the First and Only Cow grazed upon forests as if they were grass; and as for the First and Only Elephant, the rocks that she flung aside with her feet became mountains.

All these animals lived in peace, causing no harm, save for one, and that was the First and Only Crab. Now this Crab was not like the crabs we see today, but like a great fish, as tall as the smoke of three volcanoes; and she lived in a deep, deep hole at the bottom of the sea. When she went out to look for food the waters rushed into her hole, and the sea drew back from the shore; and when she came home again the sea rose again suddenly. And all this happened many times a day without order or reason, so that the fishermen of the islands could not set their nets, or their wives gather seaweed, or their little children play safely upon the beaches.

Now when He-Who-Made-All-Things saw this, he went down to the sea and called upon the First and Only Crab, telling her that henceforth she

must stay in her hole, so that the people of the islands might live in peace.

"I cannot do that," replied the Crab, "for I should starve to death. Even as it is, I am always hungry and in fear of the sharks and dogfish."

"Then you must order your times of coming and going," said He-Who-Made-All-Things. "Once a day and once a night only you must go out to find food, and no more." But the Crab looked at him and said nothing.

"If you will do as I say," said He-Who-Made-All-Things, "you and your children and your children's children shall have hard shells upon your backs, so that the sharks and the dogfish may not hurt you." But the Crab looked at him and said nothing.

"If you will do as I say," went on He-Who-Made-All-Things, "you and your children and your children's children shall have legs, so that you may go upon the land as well as in the sea." But the Crab looked at him and said nothing.

"And if you will do as I say," continued He-Who-Made-All-Things, "you and your children and your children's children shall have strong scissor claws, so that you may crack coco-nuts and eat their meat, and climb trees, and dig holes in the sand, so that both land and sea shall be safe for you."

"So be it," said the First and Only Crab.

Then He-Who-Made-All-Things was content; and he set in the sky a *Crab* made of stars, so that she should not forget her part of the bargain. And since that time all crabs have hard shells and strong scissor claws, and can go upon land as well as in the water. And the First and Only Crab leaves her hole at the bottom of the sea once each day and once each night to look for food, as she promised; but since she is lazy, each day and each night she waits a little longer, so that the tides are an hour later.

The Ram

In the beginning God made the world, and created all living things. The Devil, who had been watching, thought that now he too would create some beast. So he fashioned out of clay a long-tailed woolly ram, with curly horns and cloven hooves like his own, and tried to bring it to life; but all in vain. For two days he walked round the ram, pinching it and crying "Hey, Hey!" but the animal would not move.

Now about this time God came down to earth. He sought out Adam and Eve, and asked them how the world that he had made was getting on. They replied that everything was going well with them, but that the Devil had been boasting that he could create a beast far more beautiful than those God had made. The day before yesterday, they said, the Devil had shaped a thing called a ram out of clay, and since then he had been walking round it, pinching and poking it, and continually shouting at it "Hey, Hey!" but the ram had not moved an inch.

God roared with laughter, and asked Adam and Eve to show him the ram. When they came there, God said to the Devil, "Well, how are you getting on?"

"Badly," answered the Devil. "I have been

walking round and round this thing for two days, but it will not budge."

"I can give it life, if you like," said God. "But if I do so it must belong to me."

"Very well," said the Devil.

The Devil stood behind the ram and took hold of its long tail, while God placed himself at its head. He touched the ram with his finger and said, "Hey, Hey." The ram at once cried "Baaa!" and began running about. But its tail was left behind in the Devil's hand and did not come to life; and since that time all sheep have had stumpy tails. So that mankind would remember what had happened when the Devil tried to create life, God said that he would place the sign of the *Ram* in the sky.

The Swan

Once in Greece there lived a youth called Phaethon, who was the son of Helios the sun god and a mortal woman. Yet some of Phaethon's companions did not believe that he was of divine descent, and mocked him for saying so. He asked his mother for proof, but she could not satisfy him. So he determined to go and seek his father, though his friend Cygnus tried to discourage him, saying that the quest was too dangerous.

Phaethon travelled long and far, through many perils, and at last he came to the golden palace of the sun, where Helios sat upon his throne crowned with light. He knelt before his father and asked for some proof of his descent. "Ask whatever you like, my son," said Helios smiling, "and I swear you shall have it."

"Very well," answered Phaethon. "Let me drive your chariot for one day."

Helios was horrified, and told Phaethon that it was not possible for a mortal, or indeed for any of the other gods, even mighty Zeus, to drive the chariot of the sun. He begged Phaethon to release him from his promise, but the boy refused. So at last with many sighs Helios agreed.

Eos, the goddess of the dawn, opened the doors of heaven, and Phaethon mounted the fiery chariot. After trying once more to persuade him to give up his rash desire, Helios pointed out to his son the track that he must follow through the sky, telling him to take a middle way between the poles and not to mount too high or sink too near the earth. But Phaethon, impatient to be off, hardly listened; he only urged the four winged horses forward.

Now as the horses of the sun galloped across the sky they felt that the chariot was not so heavy as usual, or the reins so tight, and they began to plunge and rear, frightening the boy. Moreover, as he hurtled through the sky he saw that it was full of dangerous creatures. The Water-Serpent hissed at him, the two Bears and the Lion roared, the Bull lowered his head to charge, while the Scorpion raised its poisoned tail as if to sting him.

Frightened, Phaethon let the reins fall, and the horses, uncontrolled, pulled the chariot off its track and galloped wildly through the heavens. They mounted aloft, crashing against the stars; then they swooped downwards. As they neared the earth the mountains spouted fire and smoke, fields and woods were scorched, and rivers boiled in their beds; crops withered and beasts perished. Phaethon, dizzy with the heat and smoke, fainted away; his bright hair caught fire and began to burn like a torch.

Then Zeus the king of the gods rose up and, lest the world be destroyed, he hurled a thunderbolt at the chariot of the sun, so that it was broken and scattered. Phaethon, burning, fell to earth as a shooting star and plunged into the river Eridanus, which quenched his fire.

Cygnus, who mourned his friend and wished to give his body a proper burial, dived into the river again and again for many days until he had collected all Phaethon's bones. Zeus was moved by his patient search, and so that it should be remembered he placed in the sky the sign of the *Swan*, which dips its head continually into the water as Cygnus had done.

The Whale

There was once a man called Jonah who had the gift of speech. The Lord appeared to him in a dream, telling him to arise and go to the great city of Nineveh and preach there, so that the people of the city might turn from their evil ways. But Jonah did not want to do as the Lord had bid him. Instead of going to Nineveh he ran away as fast as he could in the opposite direction, towards the nearest seaport, where he found a ship that was about to set sail for a distant country. He paid his fare and went aboard, where he hid below decks to escape the sight of the Lord.

But the Lord saw Jonah nevertheless; and as the ship went over the sea he sent a great storm upon it, so that the waves rose high all around. The sailors were afraid, and each one prayed to his own god to save them, but the storm continued. Then the captain went down to where Jonah lay asleep, or seeming to sleep, and cried to him, "Oh sleeper, arise! Call upon your god, that we may not be destroyed."

Meanwhile the tempest did not cease, but grew worse, and the waves rose higher. The sailors said to each other, "Let us cast lots, so that we may know who is the cause of this great storm." So they cast lots, and the lot fell upon Jonah.

Then at last Jonah saw that he could not escape
the Lord, and he told the sailors that it was because of him that the tempest had come upon
them, and that if they hoped to be saved they must
throw him into the sea. At first they did not want
to do this, for they were good men. But the storm
grew so great that the ship seemed about to break
in two, so that they would all be drowned, and at
last they picked Jonah up and threw him over-
board. Instantly the winds ceased, and the waves
were still.

Jonah sank down and down into the sea; the
waters closed over him and the seaweed wrapped
round him. But he was not drowned, for the Lord
sent a great whale to swallow him up and save his
life. For three days and three nights he lay in the
dark belly of the whale, praying to the Lord, and
on the third day the Lord spoke to the whale, and
it swam to shore and cast Jonah out onto the sand.

Then Jonah went to the evil city of Nineveh and
preached to the people as the Lord had bade him,
and many were saved by hearing his words. And
the great *Whale* which had swallowed Jonah and
cast him out as the Lord commanded was raised
into the heavens among the stars.

The Fishes

Many years ago in America, on the southern shore of Lake Superior, there lived an Indian clan called the Fish. They were like men and women in every way, save that they had the tails of fishes. Odschig, their chief, was a brave man and strong in battle, for no arrow or spear could wound him except in one small spot at the tip of his tail. He was wise as well, and a notable hunter; though at this time it was no easy thing to find game, for it was always winter upon the earth. All the year long the trees were bare and the snow lay deep upon the ground and a cold wind blew across the frozen lake.

Now Odschig the Fish had a son who, though he was only thirteen years old, promised to be as fine a hunter as his father. But he was often unsuccessful, and though he searched all day long through the forest till his fingers were so stiff and cold that he could not string his bow, many times he came home empty-handed.

Late one afternoon, after a long and useless hunt, he leaned against the trunk of a tree to rest. As he stood there he saw a red squirrel chewing on a dried pine-cone. He was about to shoot it when it spoke to him.

"Don't kill me, son of Odschig," said the squirrel,

"but listen to my words. There is a way to end this cold and melt the snow so that you and all your tribe may have more game than you can shoot, and I who am almost dead of hunger may become fat. You must go home now, throw away your bow and arrows, and lie down in the corner and weep. You must refuse to eat or to drink, and when your father asks what it is that you want, you must say that you want him to bring you the summer out of the sky."

Odschig's son did as the squirrel had told him. "That is a hard thing to ask," his father said. "But I will get it for you if I can." So he gathered the best hunters of his tribe, and they set forth. For twenty days they walked through the thick snowy forest, and for twenty more over the ice-covered plains. At last one evening when they were so cold and hungry and weary that they could go no further they came to a mountain that seemed almost to touch the sky.

Odschig the Fish and his companions rested that night, and the next day they climbed the mountain. When they reached the top, they saw that the sky was near enough to jump into. Odschig's friend Otter jumped first. He hit his head on the sky and fell down the mountainside. "I have had enough of this," he said, and he turned and started home. Beaver jumped next, and the same thing happened to him.

Then Odschig the Fish jumped. He too was unsuccessful, but he did not lose courage and tried again, and this time a crack appeared in the sky. For his last jump Odschig gathered all his strength. He broke a great hole in the sky, into which he and his companions sprang. They found themselves on a great plain covered with grass and flowers as far as they could see. The air was soft and very warm, and the rivers full of clear water. Beasts of all sorts were there, and birds sang in the trees.

As Odschig the Fish and his companions walked across the heavens the air grew cooler, for it was leaking out through the hole he had made. The sky people began to feel cold, and some of them hid in their houses; but others who were less foolish ran to block up the hole. But by the time they got there, six months of summer had escaped, and they were only just in time to save the rest.

Odschig's companions saw the sky people coming, and managed to spring back through the hole onto the mountain. But Odschig the Fish was not so lucky. When he reached the hole it was already closed and surrounded by angry sky people. He ran away, but they pursued him across the endless plains of heaven, shooting at him with spears and arrows like a hunted animal. But their weapons only hit Odschig and fell to the ground without hurting him, and he ran on. At last, just as evening was falling and the sky people were about to give up and turn back, an arrow struck the tip of his tail, and gave him a fatal wound.

Alone in the heavens, Odschig the Fish lay down to die, saying, "My son, I have kept my promise to you, though it has cost my life. But I go in peace, for I know that now all men and beasts will be free of the cold and the snow for half of each year." So he passed away; and as it grew dark the sign of the *Fishes* appeared where he lay, as it can be seen to this time.

The Bull

In ancient times, on the seacoast of Phoenicia, there lived a princess called Europa, who was the daughter of King Agenor. One spring day she and her maidens went down to the shore to gather flowers for the palace. Zeus, who in those days often walked on earth among men, saw them, and was struck with Europa's beauty and grace. In order to approach without frightening her, he transformed himself into a great white bull and joined King Agenor's herd, which was grazing nearby.

Presently Europa and her maidens noticed the handsome new bull browsing among her father's cows by the shore. He looked at them so gently and seemed so tame that they were not afraid when he came near. Europa stroked his soft muzzle, and he knelt before her and bowed his head, lowing softly. She and her companions were charmed. They petted the bull and played with him; they wove him a wreath and a bridle of spring flowers, and led him about the meadow, while some of the most daring rode upon his broad back.

But when Europa herself mounted upon the bull's back, he reared up suddenly, galloped over the shore, and sprang into the waves, carrying her with him. He swam across the sea to the island of

Crete, where after many adventures Europa married Minos, the King of Crete, and, some say, became the mother of the Minotaur, who was half bull and half man. The divine *Bull* whose shape Zeus took can be seen today in the northern sky.

The Wolf

O nce long ago the world became so wicked that God decided to send a great flood and destroy it. But so that the races of men and beasts might be preserved, he spoke to a good man called Noah, telling him to build an Ark, and take into it his wife and family, and a pair of every kind of beast and bird.

Now when Noah had done as he was commanded the lightning began to flash and the thunder to roar and the rain to fall, and so it continued day after day until the water had covered the highest mountains. But the Ark floated safely upon the waves. And God sent angels to watch over its voyage, one for each creature, so that they might live in peace together, and that the lion might not spring upon and devour the ox, nor the eagle the dove, nor the wolf the sheep. At last the rain ceased, the waters sank, and the sky became bright again. The Ark came to rest on dry land, and Noah opened its doors so that the animals might come out.

Now the angel whose task it was to watch over the wolf looked aside for a moment; and while she did so, the wolf leaped upon the ram and killed it. The angel who watched over the sheep was angry, and said that they must destroy the wolf and his

mate. But the other angels would not agree to this, for they remembered how God had told them that he would create no more beasts, and they must therefore preserve these.

While the angels were quarrelling God appeared among them in his glory. He spoke to the angel of the sheep, telling her not to mourn for though her ram was gone, her ewe would soon give birth to twin lambs, a male and a female, and their race would be preserved until the end of time.

Then God spoke to the wolf, saying "From this time on you are accursed. You shall hide from the light of day and hunt by night, and the hand of every man shall be against you." And so it was. And God placed the signs of the Ram and the *Wolf* in the sky among the stars, that their story should not be forgotten.

The Sea-Goat

The god Pan, who dwelt in the hills and woods of Arcadia, was the protector of shepherds and herdsmen and their flocks. He saw the mountain nymph Syrinx, and fell in love with her; but she was shy and greatly feared all men. She would not stay to listen to his words of love, but ran away, and Pan ran after her. So Syrinx fled through the wilderness until she came to a deep river and could go no further. Seeing that Pan would soon be upon her, she cried out to her sisters the river nymphs for help. They heard her, and as Pan caught her in his arms she was changed into a clump of water reeds growing at the edge of the river.

Pan, mourning his loss, cut some of the reeds and made their hollow stems into a flute. And since that time he and all the shepherds of Arcadia have played their songs on a reed pipe called a syrinx after the nymph whom he loved.

Now in these times the gods did not rule the world unchallenged, but disputed it with a race of monstrous giants called the Titans. One day Pan and the other gods were resting and feasting on the banks of the river Nile. The banquet was over, and Pan was playing upon his pipes. Suddenly they were attacked by the terrible giant Typhon, who

was as tall as a mountain and breathed smoke and flames. In order to escape him the gods turned themselves into beasts. Some fled as hares or hinds, some became birds and flew away, and others changed themselves into fish and leaped into the river.

Pan also jumped into the water, but in his terror and haste he got his spells mixed up. From the waist down he became a fish, but the upper part of him was transformed into that of a he-goat, with horns and a beard. But there was no time to recast his spell, for the giant Typhon had flung himself upon Zeus, the king of the gods, and was about to tear him apart. Pan put his syrinx to his mouth and blew such a loud and piercing note that Typhon, who was stupid and cowardly like all giants, became terrified. He released Zeus and fled far away.

In gratitude for this timely help, the king of the gods set among the stars the sign of the *Sea-Goat*, which is half goat and half fish, so that Pan's deed might always be remembered. It is visible in the southern sky near the Milky Way.

The Dove

Long ago, as has been told, God sent a great flood to drown the whole world. All living creatures perished, save for Noah and his family, and the beasts and birds which they took with them into the Ark. For forty days and forty nights the rains fell; then they ceased. The sky became clear, and slowly the waters began to sink. At last the Ark came to rest among the high rocky mountains of Ararat.

Now in those days when mariners were lost at sea they would release a bird and watch which way it flew, so that they might know if land was near. Therefore Noah opened the window of the Ark, and sent out two birds, a raven and a dove. The raven flew off and did not come back; legend says that it lighted on the floating body of a drowned man, and began to devour it.

The dove also went forth and flew to and fro all day long, yet she could find no dry land upon which to rest. In the evening she returned to the Ark, and Noah stretched out his hand and took her in.

Now when seven days and seven nights had passed, Noah opened the window of the Ark and sent forth the faithful dove again. And in the evening she returned to him with a twig from an olive tree in her mouth; and thus he knew that the waters had sunk far enough to disclose the tops of the trees.

When seven more days and nights had passed, Noah sent out the dove a third time, and that evening she did not return. Then he knew that the flood had passed, and the sun shone again upon the earth. And he opened the doors of the Ark, and the beasts and birds came forth.

God, to honour the *Dove* for her faithful service, raised her into the heavens, where she shines in the southern sky. But the faithless raven became a bird of ill-omen, and is shunned even today by all men.